When I Was a Girl Like Me

Like Me

When I Was a Girl Like Me

poems by

Margaret Bazzell-Crocker

STUBBORN MULE PRESS
DEVIL'S ELBOW, MO

Stubborn Mule Press
Devil's Elbow, MO
stubbornmulepress.com

First Edition 11 7 5 3 2 1
ISBN: 978-1-950380-12-1
LCCN: 2019935875
Design, edits and layout: Jeanette Powers
stubbornmulepress@gmail.com @stubbornmulepress
Cover Image Art: Ash Crocker
Interior Art: "Portrait of a Woman": John Smart, Nelson-Atkins
                    Museum of Art, Kansas City
Bio Photo: Daniel Crocker

When I was a girl like me
my job
wasn't what I was,
my pet wasn't what I was,
and no children called me mother.

—from 'For Carrie'

These few words and all of my heart
are for Dan ...

Introduction

An emotion that generally gets the most results is anger. People are afraid of anger and especially women are afraid to be angry.

It might be unseemly. It might cause a scene.

When I was young, I was angry a lot.

As I got older, I tried to quash this completely from me, knowing how devastatingly effective anger can be.

This only made me angrier.

I am now comfortable with my anger and, because of years of practice, I can aim it with laser precision. I am, thus, very careful with anything that truly angers me. Not irritates. Not annoys. Angers. Infuriates.

I will not be careful this time.

MBC

Contents

THE WRENCH

Our house was China once.
And yours was, too.
When the girls held your place
and the girls held their breath
until you arrived.

A boy can hold many things.
A wrench,
a gun,
a dick
and a name.

We were never equal,
you and I.
I have always lived in your shadow.

You hold my green card,
you hold my countenance,
you hold my rights, decisions and future sight,
you hold my agency,
my reproductive rights
and my freedom to move within your regions,
you hold my paycheck, my promotions and my wherewithal,
and you held my tongue.

Until now.

THE ART OF ACQUIESCENCE

To be a woman
in this world
is to bend and curve and slip around its corners
like a snake in the river.

The river has always been there,
the current
and the rocky banks,
the tangle of roots,
a snapping turtle,
a stray foot
or fish just larger than you.
Your role is not to disturb, no.
Look at you!
You have no bones to do so!

All you want is a bug,
a minnow,
a stray lizard,
sunshine
and a warm rock.
But the foot is there,
the current
and the hook.
And you will contort yourself
to meet them all.

AGE
(or)
WHAT THE HELL DO I WRITE ABOUT NOW—
AS TOLD THROUGH THE WEEKEND BINGE

FRIDAY

And drinking is a revolution
when I am first free,
when my thoughts are suddenly my own,
when the calendar is my own,
when I can quit on a dime or spit on a dollar,
when I am telling you and not being told,
when things are split, reconfigured and split again in hours, in
moments,
when there are things I have to tell you right now,
when I well know what concrete, pencil, myth and creation are,
when I walk with no leash,
shuck influence, no matter how sound,
when I ask,
when I answer,
when I am dissatisfied with the response,
when I firmly choose fight over flight.

This is when I write it all.
Because all the world should know.

SATURDAY

And drinking is a secret
when I discover
I am not free.
When my thoughts become someone else's thoughts,
when days are minutes, hours and wooden blocks of time I carry

to give to someone else,
when children come or not come,
grow or not grow
and the anxiety is felt or not felt,
depending.
When you are thus mother or father
or you are not,
when you talk to your mother or father
or not,
when you compare many things,
when you attend conferences and pay attention because that is
what adults do,
when you contemplate church,
when your progeny is on the vine and you are unsure what the
harvesting process is,
when things are harder than they should be,
when you're making it,
when you're barely making it,
when people rely on you and you don't rely on you.

That is when I write what I can.
And, only for me.

SUNDAY

And drinking is something I've earned, dammit,
when I've taken care of the things I can see,
when I've worried about things I can't,
when people won't care or believe,
when I question myself,
when I have the wrong answers,
when I answer anyway,
when I've done my share,
when I plainly see injustice I extol upon but not fix,
when you have a point of view,
when I have a point of view,
when I am felt,

like weather,
and disregarded,
when I must clean up and make amends,
when I fully understand the consequences,
and when I am cleaning this mess I've created on Friday.

And when you, me and Lionel Richie are all wondering,
what the hell do I write about now?

GROWING UP
CURRY-KELLY-BAZZELL-KINCAID-HASTY-CROCKER:
A GUIDE FOR THE BEGINNER

Welcome to the enclave!
We know it can be nerve-wracking during your first days,
or even during any of the subsequent days of your stay!
It's okay if you feel disoriented.
Many women have come before you.
We know you have questions about the steps toward your
eventual acceptance of our program,
so we've created this helpful guide to assist you!

If you are a Curry,
you may not even be aware of it,
as you have been taken by a "nurse"
and quickly placed into Kelly care.
You may ignore this step
until age 15,
when you will suddenly be aware
that this step
was probably a necessary one.

If you are a Kelly,
DON'T TOUCH THAT,
and,
CAN'T YOU TAKE THEM OUTSIDE.
These are not moments we touch,
these are not events
we touch,
our face is fragile,
our facade is fragile,
our inclusion is fragile and it comes with conditions,
and you,
my dear,
are walking on eggshells.

If you are a Bazzell,
okay then!
There's some crazy going on there, and that's okay!
We understand.
Please deposit any metal objects into the receptacle to your right
and remove your hard-soled shoes.
We apologize,
but your history is incomplete.
We cannot process.

If you are a Kincaid,
see appendix B (If You Are A Kincaid).
Remember that we know what you are feeling
even though we may or may not be able to communicate with you now,
depending on the will of your captor.
Please see your male Kincaid supervisor for more information.

If you are a Hasty,
you've become part of what can only be described as a "mixed bag."
Things have happened
medically,
socially,
emotionally
and even legally.
It's alright.
We have a helpline dedicated just for you.
Injured on a Mississippi barge line?
Have an inactive or non participatory mother?
Do you suffer from kidney stones?
Have you or a loved one ever been estranged?
All of our attendants are currently helping other customers.
While you're waiting,
try some alcohol,
12 Hail Mary's,
an AA meeting and another relapse,
$1000.00 bond,
your face in the Daily Journal
and a photo of the child you've sponsored in South America.

If you are a Crocker,
congratulations!
You've made it through!
And I'll bet you've made several friends along the way!
As a Crocker,
you've attended some deaths,
and you may have come to realize how tenuous a life is,
how gossamer,
how we all share a thin cocoon,
how glassine these threads become when we spit on cotton,
the wind
and fate itself to get away from the web,
only to wrap ourselves further in it,
like mummies who've pronounced themselves devoid of the Nile.
Of course the river loves you, the waters say.

If you are a Crocker,
you've broken new ground
and shaken old ground, too,
for there is not a way you have not suffered,
there is not a tomb
you have not cooked a casserole to commemorate.
You have seen death,
you have drank coffee.

And you are not afraid.

DÖSTÄDNING

We grew up poor,
married poor,
raised children poor,
went to school poor,
had three jobs apiece,
sold things at the pawn shops and bought them back,
only to sell them again for food,
toilet paper,
toothpaste
and diapers.

We had bills we chose to pay,
and bills that haunt us still.
We ate things from a can that should never be canned,
when our lives were *Döstädning*, morning to night
and morning again.

We are only beginning now to understand possession
and the pride of it
when you tell me that minimalism
is all the rage.

Tell a stray cat
about all you discovered during your *Döstädning*.
Tell a torn backpack on the highway,
a shoe on a high wire,
my pawn shop receipt.
Tell my W.I.C. vouchers about how decluttering my life,
and realizing how close to death we really are
will make me
and my children
fulfilled.

THE DUCK AT THE PARK

The duck at the park
is a carnival on dead trees.
Its ass is a *sproing* the children spring back and forth,
anchored in pebbles
and overhung
by the giant caterpillar,
the smiling caterpillar
that everyone on the Optimists Club Committee
thought was just utterly "too-too,"
the only club in Cape
that refuses to discuss the End Times.

Forty-two years of young riders
have taken layers of the duck's skin and seat
home on their pants,
revealing like an Everlasting Gobstopper
uneven rings of primer and touch-up
beneath still,
as gaudy as greasepaint
in sun and wind,
like a flower that smells better as it rots.

The duck at the park
is set apart from other recreational metalwork
like an afterthought,
and my kids have a love/hate relationship with it.
In August, the duck developed wasps
and now my daughters wait and watch
with the seriousness of foremen
as I test each piece of park tomfoolery.
Kick and retreat.
Wait.
Kick and retreat.
Okay.

Today I have sketched the duck in the park,
the duck that with living ducks flying on my perspective,
seems more alive by color and movement,
and I've drawn it to remind me
that living is not fading,
and living is not sitting on a rusty coil in rocks
and waiting for anything to move you,
it's being dangerous sometimes
to those who least expect it
and myself, too,
and living is bending a little more
and exposing myself to come-what-may.

The duck at the park,
inert as it may seem,
has a life
I've placed my own upon,
throwing my own weight backwards and forwards
and laughing
while my children watch
and wonder
who will break first?
The duck?
Me?

THIS IS A SOFT DEATH

I am delighted,
the dog is delighted,
all the school children are delighted
at the first big snow.

Our dog, Charlie, explores.
He's never seen it,
heard the muffling effects of it,
how well he and I can hear everything from blocks away,
he smells it,
smells it,
snuffles it
and smells it again,
runs races around it,
and challenges it in the yard.

They are big,
white flakes,
that fool us all into holiness.

The first snow covers everything
in something new.
This isn't just a flurry,
but an actual cleansing,
an obliteration from brown to gray to white in seconds,
and we shovel the cleansing away,
and we shovel again when we realize snow is still coming down
and we shovel
into the night we shovel,
and in the morning,
whether we want it or not,
we must push it aside
to start anew.

Goddammit, we must all start anew.

MENTAL HEALTH— PORTRAIT 1

Offices are silent
and locked at night.

And bland doors upon doors
and myself,
white and nervous against the glass
broken with chickenwire.

The pads of my shoes are quiet.
The elevator's shaky hum is quiet.
The shadows of the dining hall are quiet and long.
The dust on the carcass of a water beetle,
the saw that does not move,
the razor behind the lock,
the fingers,
stained with marker,
and clenched in state blankets.

The voices
are silent
while a reflection of me
smokes in the yard.

MENTAL HEALTH— PORTRAIT 2

Cee Cee
smiling in the hall.
She rubs her forehead back and forth,
her fingers back and forth,
the air twisting
her knuckles back and forth,
flies rubbing.

Cee Cee
taking a shower.
Her t-shirt is hung
empty on the door.

Cee Cee in line
waiting for that Red Cross t-shirt,
a souvenir of another life
of outside
and pursuits she sleeps away here,
of a time she had something to give.

Cee Cee in line
with a Dixie cup of orange juice
and that crazy, crazy blood
pumping a hole through the universe,
her head
bumping softly at the wall
again
again
as she stares past the door.

A sticker, a lollipop and a smiley-face on the board,
this is what she has now.

Cee Cee
carrying a cheap comb in a paper bag.

Cee Cee watches the bored nurse
and today's group discussion
"To Cope or Not To Cope."

That is the question.

THE DAYS OF MY DEATH

"No one escapes life alive."
                    —African proverb

"What the fuck?"
                    —some guy, dying

Today is the day I will die.

In the dark,
the alarm,
and my feet find themselves to lead me through the gauntlet,
black ceiling,
static,
sleeping fur at my toes,
sharp edges,
a blurry light in the field of my vision,
feet slide,
fingers shuffle,
searching, feeling, bumping, frantic,
to stop the noise.
Stop the noise.

I am awake.

There are screens then,
to show me pretty pictures,
to label things correct, alarming or DEFCON 4.
Internal lists begin to re-establish their hold,
I pull on my clothes
and begin, again to enter the land of the living
and show,
with good grooming,
how civilized I can be.

Work is work.
I don't push a barrow,
I don't harvest this winter's pantry,
I don't kill, cure or stretch hides.
I fill forty hours to receive weekly paper
vaguely related to the gold standard,
the Illuminati or Ancient Aliens.
Whichever.

It is evening.
The kids are gone,
my man is asleep
and only the cats remain.
My god.
Where did we get so many cats?
Everyone knows they steal your breath,
they're unlucky,
they like the number 13,
they're born with a middle paw straight to the heavens
and two feet in the grave
and they're always watching,
watching to see what we will give.

I have nothing.
I gave at the office,
feet and fingers and brain.

The evening is a beer,
warm water
and more pretty, moving pictures to oblivion.
And then, tomorrow.

Tomorrow is the day I will die.

WINNING THE MEGA MILLIONS

Dear God.

Back in the day,
there was a way to get to You.
A lamb,
a certain cut of hair,
a single-fiber garment that would woo You my way.
We used to know
from stones,
from bones,
from blood
and from flaming plants
what You wanted,
what You needed from us
in a world where all of us were heard,
You,
the faithful,
the dead,
the rocks
and even the burning bush.

I don't know You anymore.
I can't feel You.

But I bought this Mega Millions ticket
hoping You would be there,
I have no lamb.
I have no hair,
I've burnt everything and saved nothing for You,
not even the ashes.
I've eaten the bread because it is all we have to eat,
and I've been swallowed by the whale many times over.

Still now,
I have saved for You
the stones,
the bones,
the blood,
and all these flaming plants You desire,
only to hold a losing ticket.

MODERN ALCHEMY

I make 2.5 cents every minute I sit here,
and I have never been more aware
of each quarter of a fifth
of one half cent
that ticks by.

And yet,
how quickly it goes,
like tickets at the fair,
when time is changed
to money
in my hands.

MOON AND ELEPHANT

Women,
flat-footed, gray
and ivory-toothed,
do not forget.
Women remember
a cut from 1994,
and the flowers you sent yesterday.
We dwell in them,
bleeding from night to turning night
in the nettles
(is she right? am I only that?)
or rolling naked in the petals
(of course he should buy me flowers. everyone should buy me flowers.)
rising and falling
(did he say that? what did she mean?)
in a clear glass on the windowsill.

Sylvia Plath was quiet.
Even her husband didn't know she wasn't cooking that day.
The rest is flowers
or thorns,
someone asking what the hell happened,
an open oven door,
the memory of an elephant
and an orange moon in August
above the car.

PRISON

It is women who civilize the world
I think,
searching cells upon cells
of men left to other men's devices,
of long numbers and gray shirts like lemming skins,
of dried beef stew from canteen,
of static chairs and phones in naked rows
and showers for God and everyone.

A man can torment a man.

With sharp lights that never change,
soft shoes
and the rationing of toilet paper.
ALL IS SAFE.
GO BACK TO YOUR HOMES NOW.
We have caged the predators.

The men have things to break the men,
thin bars of soap,
flip flops
and thermostats five degrees too short,
a marked lack of red meat,
concrete floors and metal tables,
soft rubber spoons
and an eternal light for their closed eyes.
The eternal light of the Just
have men.

And me,
searching cells upon cells of dirty dim atrocities
and fussing with doilies at home
to cover everything uncivilized in lace.

A BARREN TREE
WITH A DRIED SPARROW'S NEST
NEAR A DESOLATE SOUP
OF STRANGE BIOLOGY

We are going to get Marcus.

Marcus speaks in television commercials.
"We'll be right back!"
he says,
over and over.

And we will.

After these brief messages.

When people get older, they talk.
People who have hated people for years
get older
and talk to the people they hate
in an agony
of confession.

They need to tell you everything.

I
will tell you everything.

In Missouri, there is a town called Rockville
which sits at the bottom of the only plinth of rock
in a wide neighborhood of prairie.
The rock is a mammoth wall
against the town,
and the town
a sniveling footnote to its very existence.
In the shadow of this rock,
upon which a pair of actual fucking eagles nest,

human things
also actually exist, if you can believe it.
Trains arrive and depart.
Chickens feed.
Humans love and do not love.
Goats and donkeys do not graze, but are fed,
as reliant upon schedules as you and I.

Think about that,
for a moment.

Your schedule
and a donkey's schedule
are probably the same.

The van lumbers over railroad tracks,
past bare fields
and the detritus from the one and only
rocky crag above,
as we collect Marcus from his home
at the base of what was once,
surely,
a place of worship and awe.
"I'm loving it!"
he tells us
as we guide him into his seat,
one bare cliff towering above us in smooth detachment
from the fleas at its base.
We pull out of his driveway
to face the genetic engineering company
opposite the sparse settlement of Rockville
and see
a barren tree
with a dried sparrow's nest
near a desolate soup
of strange biology
in the long fallow ground
between the factory
and God.

I CANNOT LIVE WITHOUT YOU

How can I live without you?
Or you?
Or you,
when I have been trained to need you,
to bind you,
to bear you,
to love you and stand with you,
and to heal all things within you?

There are no mirrors that reflect only me,
no decisions I make without first thinking about all of us,
nothing I love
more than everything
animals,
children,
plants,
families,
togetherness,
justice
and unicorns.

I cannot live without you,
because I am ingrained in you.
because I am flipping a coin to make your decisions,
because my decisions are not enough for you,
because I am remembering my mother,
your mother,
the family unit,
and everything in our future.
I am accommodating,
mingling,
negotiating,
and bringing the hostages home.

I am always bringing the hostages home.

FOR CARRIE

I am of an age,
many things do not astound me.
I am in the new bracket,
mine eyes have been opened.
I drive the gray car to a cream office
work a tan day
and dream in taupe and robin's-egg-blue.
I speak 1-dog 2-kid small-town big-fence talk,
and I forget
there were ever girls like me
that saw girls like me
like giants.

When I was a girl like me
my job
wasn't what I was,
my pet
wasn't what I was,
and no children called me mother.
I saw red,
drank stout,
lived black, black nights
and half days of lists of mother's unrealized dreams,
and more were coming after me
in thick films of peanut-shaped pictures
with no cigar-smoking back-slapping appendages,
more girls
I knew
would love the whiskey like I did,
would mourn the father that could have been.
More to live red and black
and wonder what the hell a man really looked like,
more to see the unit falter again and again,
more to look hard
and crumble every day.

And one,
one girl like me,
when I was a girl like me,
a girl who turned the ashes and found a feather,
a woman
who hugged me tonight
and made me dream of fenceless acres
of green,
green,
green.

EARTH, AIR AND LYNDA CARTER

I first remember flying.

Flying

with the ceiling's 70's popcorn textures
at my cheek.
I could touch it
if I'd only stretched out my hand.

I was a superhero then,
in my first moments of life and memory,
with my Wonder Woman Underoos,
Lasso of Truth
and the bad guy in the background
for seconds,
long particles of seconds,
an eternity of nanoseconds,
in Million Dollar Man slow motion,
with the Bionic Woman smiling at my shoulder.

"Forget Lee Majors,"
she whispers,
"and fuck the Army.
Let's leave it all behind with our invisible jet."

And then I land,

remembering landing for the first time,
as I remember no other landings before now.
The Underoos ruck up to my armpits,
everything explodes,
the house explodes,
sound and sight explode,
the air, Lynda Carter
and Lindsay Wagner are sucked from my universe,

the villain is there,
and the ultimate final twist—

That our heroine
could never fly,
after all.

TWO IN THE SMOKING SECTION

The fly lights on broken dishes,
only he is gentle here.
The food a wave's crust,
the garbage spears,
the shattered ashes,
the rusted clumps of scum,
all are caressed by his wing.
The molded holes of fruit pits,
the running meat,
the ruined young of birds,
the rotting papers,
all are solid by his feathered arm
and by mine.

I watch
and gather his crushed brethren around me,
crying,
for now they do not help he and I
to consume this buffet
of error and fickle use.

LOVE POEM 4

Dog barking
in the dark.
My husband's shoulder
like Achilles'
stretches unattended.
Blinds
to Orion,
Sagittarius, the Archer,
as I sink to a bed whose spring is gone
dreaming
that the oak
also protects the moss.

THE PERIOD PIECE

She is always accompanied
wherever she goes.
Her speech is heard,
her thoughts are measured,
her every whim and interest are all of ours to admire.
And to monitor.

She is precious
like a diamond,
rare as an orchid,
tiny as a laughing child.
She is this metaphor and that simile,
and we love her for how she can contrast and compare
with things we are comfortable admiring.

But we do not admire her,
no.
Why would you think such a thing?
We only speak to placate her by flowers,
because
she likes children,
and kittens,
and comforting creatures such as ourselves,
who fight
and bruise
and quash
and censor
and decide for
and watch with squinted eyes
and listen.

We listen very closely
to ensure
she does not rise again.

THE TEST

You and I do not think
about pumping blood,
beating heart,
bowels,
breasts or bile
until the needle is come,
the CAT scan
or the sonographer's stare
at a fuzzy screen we cannot decipher.

Only when the stethoscope's chill
touches our skin
do we think about breath and life,
praise it,
pray for its everlasting grace,
wonder at its every hitch and cough
and count our mortal breaths until the ending.

TIME, TEA AND WATER

There are slow things here.

Sleep,
waiting rooms,
cooking stew,
comparing car prices,
waiting for a bread to rise
or water to boil.
Tea is slow
and perfect.

But time
is not slow.
Time will drag your face and mine
and the memory of your face and mine
through sand
with a willow twig.
None will stay.

None will stay.

But, there are slow things.
Gardening,
canning,
the birth, potty training and death of a dog you've loved,
a dog who,
in the end,
pissed on your best rug
and you still loved him to infinity
and wished for him a million rugs just for pissing on,
the ages of daughters,
the perfect cup of tea.

Floods come often here.

Sometimes,
they are bright black, raging rivers
followed by the whole tri-county KFVS-12 viewing area.
Maps shown, sirens sound, alerts declared.
And sometimes, the floods are measured, steady and insidious
until they are over your doorstep.

ME,
AND THE HECATE

Ariadne,
in the mechanical bed,
bound by stuffed mittens,
breathing by beeping hose,
her pulse rate, heart rate, brain rhythms and lung capacities
a constellation around us in the darkened room.
There are stars, Ariadne!
Look!

Ariadne,
your webs.

Ariadne,
your unrequited love.

You were our lives,
Ariadne,
and your webs our ties with you,
you the weaver,
you the hanged man,
you the Hecate,
the maid, mother and crone all in one
a white, fragile web in the dark
while machines give you breath and life in force,
as you would have none on your own.

Ariadne,
what do you weave there,
where no one can see?

You wake hoarse,
confused,
and tangled in all your knitting.
You see me,

and don't remember.
But I will always remember these days, my sisters.

When Ariadne began to sew,
and faltered.

DEAR MARY,

You're better than spam, Mary.
Every time I open my email you're there
with a quote from Leviticus,
a warning that some medical jiggery
is a screw to me or my loved ones,
or an unbelievable picture
that looks like a Miracle
and smells like Photoshop.

Dear Mary,
I would tell you to save yourself the trouble
but I know those emails
probably do you more good than me.

I don't believe in God anymore, Mary.
I don't believe
in the amazing tortilla of *Guadalupe*
or that shrouds can take pictures.
I don't believe in the Easter Bunny
or the goddamned miracle of birth, Mary.
I don't believe any of that shit.
You can send me all the "Love Is" cartoons
and aww-inducing kitty pics
and real-life testimonials of doctors
who saw the blind see,
heard the deaf hear,
felt the passion of someone
who was dead inside only a moment before,
eyes widening,
chills,
and a chorus of light in my head,
surely, Mary,
surely I am witnessing a miracle, Mary,
and not slipping into something less than divine,
like greed

or fame
or a fantasy that I am the center of the universe
and all good things come unto me.

Dear Mary,
Faith is for those people stupid enough
or strong enough
to trust something they've never seen,
and if you ask me,
the stupid and the strong don't need faith anyway.
The strong will make it through
and the stupid won't know that they haven't.

As for me,
Mary,
I'll open your emails as I always do.
But I won't believe,
no matter how many
beautiful sunsets over magnificent valleys you send me,
no matter how many eternal flames,
no matter how many made it through whatever disaster,
no matter, Mary.

I won't believe again, Mary.
Not even this
one
last
time.

A NOMAD'S ROMANCING

A nomad's one truest ability
and honest desire
is the crashing.
She will sink the sandman as painlessly as possible
and mold any soft species of park-sitting wood.
A nomad easily shakes off a rough coffee
near whatever intersections,
cramps bunkless without a name to warm her,
creates unstable herds,
pitches tents right on top of Texaco stars
where its heat might once melt
the oodles of needles of shitty roads
taken in dark,
staring,
anytime hours from her rest.

The nomad's scandalous romance of the roads
and her flimsy chains of costume jewelry
all that mixing makes
is distasteful
and necessary
as the oily mechanic's stains
that settle into her niches
from right engines.
A nomad's rashing dream
is an occasional itch
for the unscratchable suburbia
she soothes
by passing through her circles,
the even trading of yin lives
for hobby yangs,
the vacation a knitting TV dinner might make
as she pauses...

She'll catch tastes of it

and wad it into a sane piece of pocket
while tucking any immediate neighbor's dailies,
like the guest sheets they are,
beneath her different chin
and awaiting the moment
the rousing morning birds talk about
when we drink our cappuccinos
and she smokes our butts
and all of us get up
and keep on going,
keep on going.

WE LIVE IN A NEW NEIGHBORHOOD NOW.
YOU CAN'T DO THAT SHIT ANY MORE.

In my head,
I was CSI: Miami once,
trying to figure out the garbage in my yard.

Who ate teriyaki peanuts?
Why is there a ferret food container in my bushes?
Who had the temerity to drink a decent wine on this corner?

Before we came to this real town with real zoning laws,
the roads
and yards were ours
and no one else's,
because no one,
long and long ago or even now,
had ever wanted that land,
ever,
that land was shit,
and we were only page holders
in that long history of cursing the reasons we were born here.

All the dogs are tethered in this neighborhood
and my days are less exciting for it.

Where once I had an alarm system,
a protocol,
several loose pets howling,
loud music,
the next door neighbor shouting,
bright lights and people gathered,
staring at a porch,
a corner,
a light in the distance,
now I have only custom-made blinds
and flags proclaiming someone's allegiance to Summer to

guide me.
Tonight,
I see a human in the distance,
the dude with no curtains across the back fences,
who drinks first from one glass and then another.
And then another again.

And suddenly I know,
without garbage,
without shouting,
without lights or loud noises,
without a guard dog,
without Girl Scout cookies,
a soundtrack,
peanuts or broken beer bottles in the yard,
he's had a hard day,
and I think
maybe, I could live
in this neighborhood.

U-HAUL

My daughters are going away.

The first time I was separated from them,
U-Haul paid the price,
as the cat and I howled,
furniture rolled
and all of us learned
what mothers can and cannot take.

We lived together then,
in rooms,
all of us,
mothers, sisters, wives and families yet to be.
Where are our rooms,
they would ask,
and we would offer a pillow,
an animal,
a cat,
a cushion,
a couch,
a floor
and a home.

Our daughters are going away.
We are inside while the storm rages,
but we are ever watchful for our girls
whose voices we hear
faintly
through the radio.

MY JOINTS HURT
AND OTHER FASCINATING TOPICS OF
CONVERSATION

And, so.

This is what it's come to.
You
and me,
green tea
and a free association of maladies.

You cannot know how sick I am,
the pain I feel,
the woes I have.

But, hey,
here's a dirty joke to make it better.

All laugh.
I cough.
You sweat.
We both sigh,
and limp
ever closer
to the finish line.

WHERE THE HEROINE LIVES IN THE END

Once upon a time,
there was a cave,
a den,
a hut,
a house
and a fire.
One of us was here
and one of us was there
and one of us was not at all.
We worshiped things,
we reviled things
and we abhorred all things.
Our hearts were whole
and they were broken.
We were waiting
doing,
planning,
dreaming
and picking up the pieces.

You and I knew things once
and we knew nothing, none of us.

We slew monsters,
bore children,
solved mysteries,
saved everyone,
lost the most important thing,
and died anyway,
in the end.

But the etchings in the rock,
the flickering lights on our rapt faces,
the click-bait,

the Lifetime movies,
the strange alphabet,
the way you lay your walls without mathematics,
the Polaroids,
the bones from all you've sacrificed,
the stairs to nowhere and everywhere,
the melodies learned by heart,
the Plasticine-wreathed crosses on every highway and every road,
the scrapbooks,
the collectibles
and the fire.
All of these are ours.

We will only, ever, die in the end.

But, the fire will make us immortal.

Margaret Bazzell-Crocker lives in Southern Missouri with her husband of 25 years and her daughters, who float in and out of her life. Margaret would like to thank several publications for celebrating her art and work; among them As It Ought To Be, the Sanesplaining podcast (of whom she is a host), Windowpanes and Green Bean Press. This is not an inclusive list. She would especially like to thank her husband, who has always loudly encouraged her to publish his favorites, and her daughters, family and friends, who have provided much inspiration and good examples of how life should be lived.

CPSIA information can be obtained
at www.ICGtesting.com
Printed in the USA
BVHW031742020419
544392BV00001B/98/P

9 781950 380121